10 CHRISTMAS DUETS VOL 1.

CONTENTS

Jingle Bells

James Pierpont
arr. B C Dockery

Jingle Bells

Jingle Bells

Jingle Bells

Flute 1

James Pierpont
arr. B C Dockery

Flute 2

Jingle Bells

James Pierpont
arr. B C Dockery

Jingle Bells

Piano

James Pierpont
arr. B C Dockery

Jingle Bells

What Child Is This (Greensleeves)

Traditional

What Child Is This (Greensleeves)

Flute 1

Traditional

What Child Is This (Greensleeves)

Flute 2

Traditional

Piano

What Child Is This (Greensleeves)

Traditional

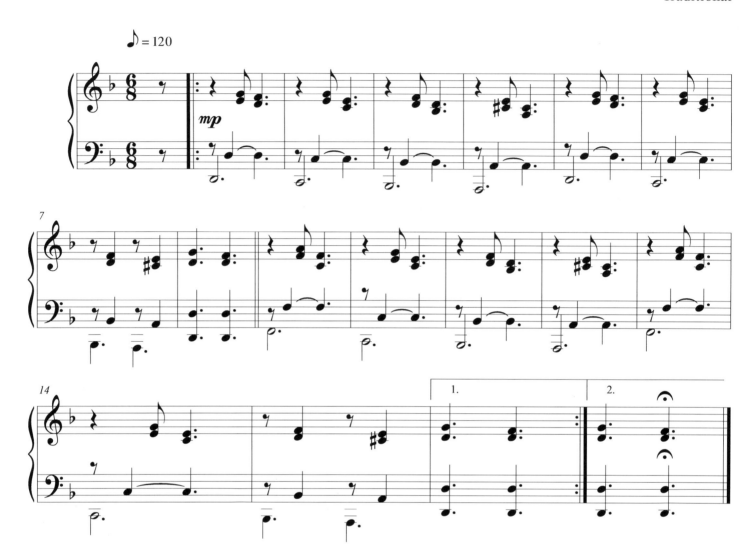

Silent Night

Franz Gruber

Silent Night

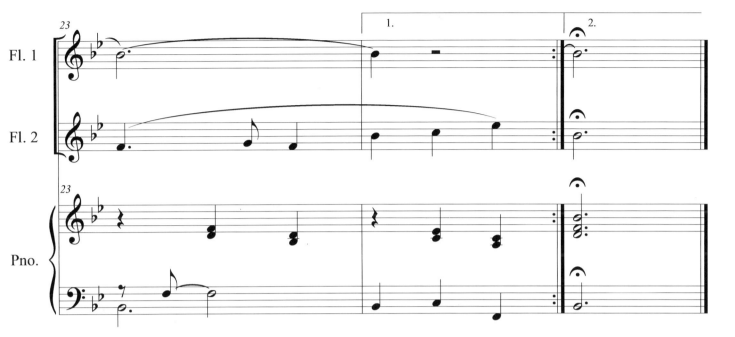

Silent Night

Flute 1

Franz Gruber

Silent Night

Flute 2

Franz Gruber

Silent Night

Piano

Franz Gruber

O Come All Ye Faithful

John Francis Wade

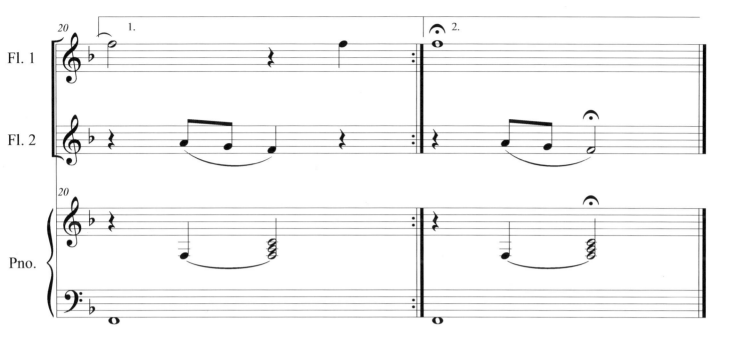

Flute 1

O Come All Ye Faithful

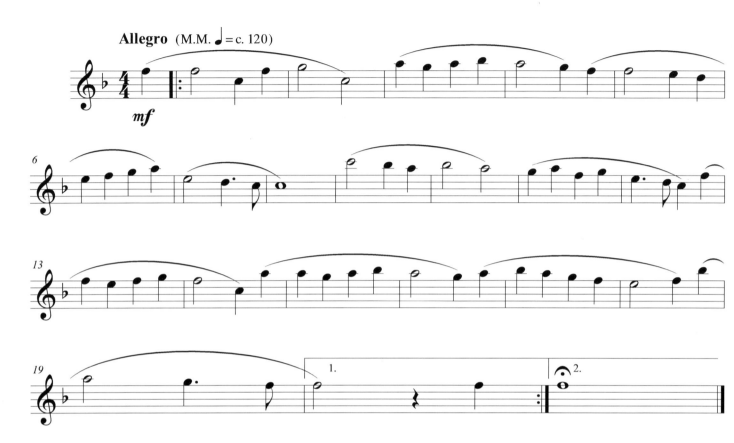

Flute 2

O Come All Ye Faithful

John Francis Wade

O Come All Ye Faithful

Piano

John Francis Wade

Allegro (M.M. ♩ = c. 120)

Joy To The World

Handel
arr. B C Dockery

Flute 1

Joy To The World

Handel
arr. B C Dockery

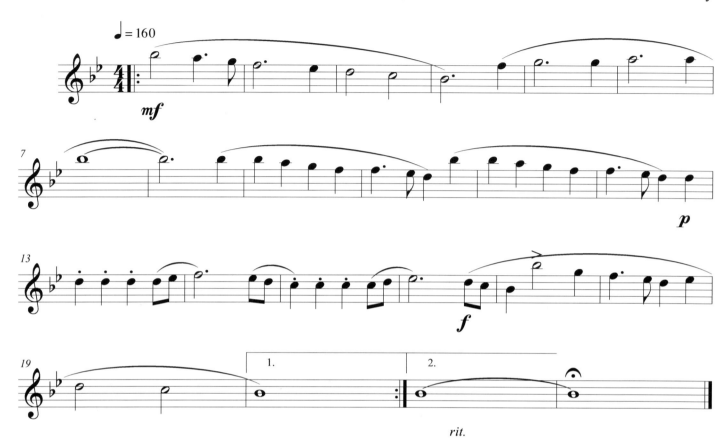

Joy To The World

Flute 2

Handel
arr. B C Dockery

Joy To The World

Piano

Handel
arr. B C Dockery

Away in a Manger

James R. Murray
arr. B C Dockery

Away in a Manger

Flute 1

James R. Murray
arr. B C Dockery

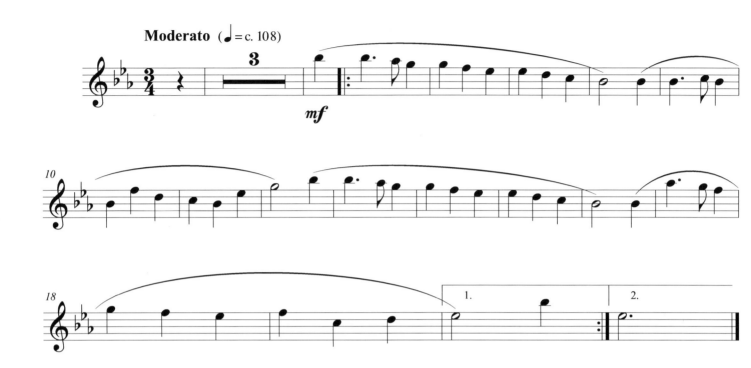

Away in a Manger

Flute 2

James R. Murray
arr. B C Dockery

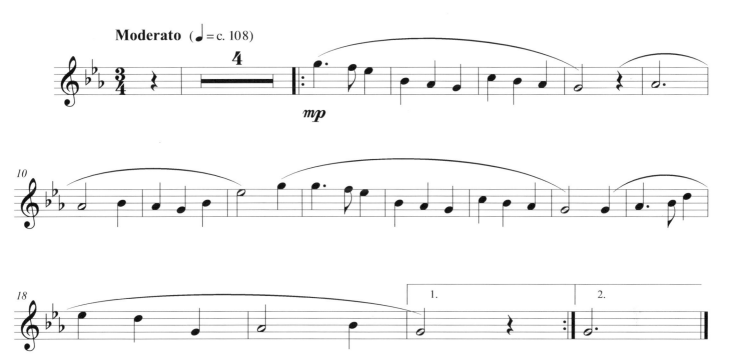

Piano

Away in a Manger

James R. Murray
arr. B C Dockery

We Three Kings

John Henry Hopkins, Jr.

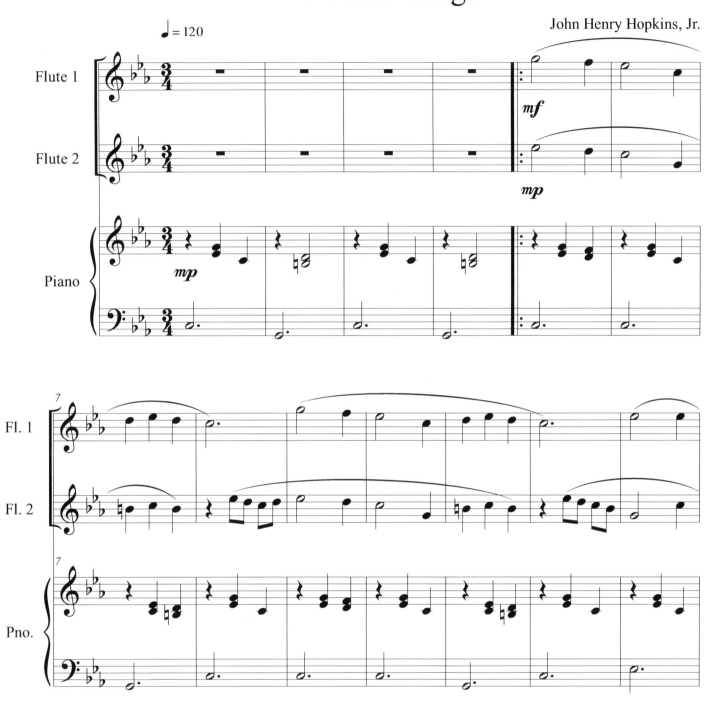

Flute 1

We Three Kings

John Henry Hopkins, Jr.

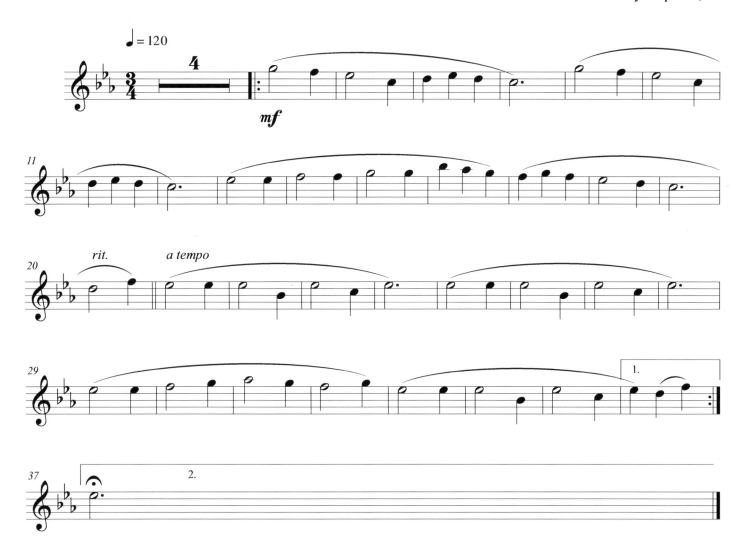

Flute 2

We Three Kings

John Henry Hopkins, Jr.

We Three Kings

Piano

John Henry Hopkins, Jr.

Away in a Manger (Cradle Song)

William J. Kirkpatrick
arr. B C Dockery

Away in a Manger (Cradle Song)

Away in a Manger (Cradle Song)

Flute 1

William J. Kirkpatrick
arr. B C Dockery

Away in a Manger (Cradle Song)

Flute 2

William J. Kirkpatrick
arr. B C Dockery

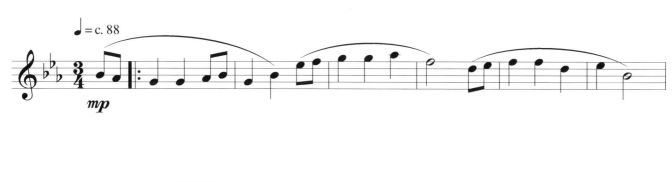

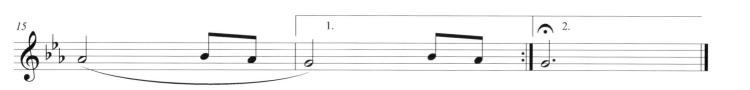

Away in a Manger (Cradle Song)

Piano

William J. Kirkpatrick
arr. B C Dockery

O Holy Night

Adolphe Adam
arr. B C Dockery

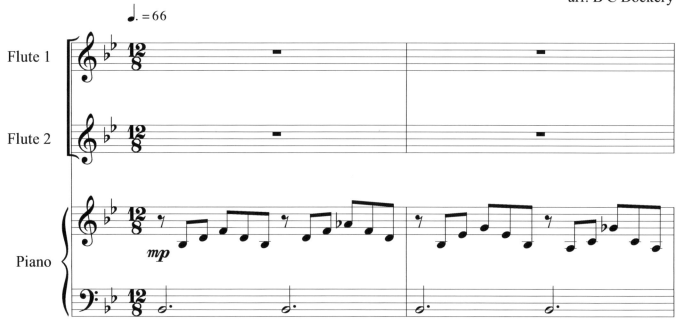

O Holy Night

O Holy Night

O Holy Night

O Holy Night

Flute 1

Adolphe Adam
arr. B C Dockery

O Holy Night

Flute 2

Adolphe Adam
arr. B C Dockery

O Holy Night

Piano

Adolphe Adam
arr. B C Dockery

O Holy Night

The First Noel

Traditional
arr. B C Dockery

The First Noel

Flute 1

Traditional
arr. B C Dockery

The First Noel

Flute 2

Traditional
arr. B C Dockery

The First Noel

Piano

Traditional
arr. B C Dockery

Made in the USA
Las Vegas, NV
23 November 2024

12488439R00039